MY SPORT
ICE SKATING

Tim Wood

Photographs: Chris Fairclough

Franklin Watts
New York • London • Sydney • Toronto

Franklin Watts Inc
387 Park Avenue South
New York
NY 10016

Printed in Italy by G. Canale & C.S.p.A. Turin

Design: K & Co

Library of Congress Cataloguing-in-Publication Data
Wood, Tim.
    Ice Skating / Tim Wood.
      p.   cm. — (My sport)
    Summary: Examines the training, preparation, and techniques
involved in figure skating.
    ISBN 0-531-14051-2
    1. Skating—Juvenile literature.   [1. Ice skating.]   I. Title.
II. Series: Wood, Tim My sport.
GV850.4.W66   1990   89-49272
796.91—dc20   CIP
                                                    AC

Illustrations: Simon Roulestone, Angela Owen

The publishers, author and photographer would
like to thank Cheryl Harris, Fiona Dickson, Bernice
Ede and the staff of Aldershot Ice Rink for their
help and cooperation in making this book.

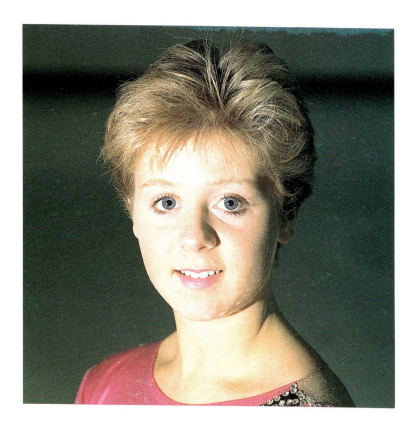

The skater featured in this book is Cheryl Harris. Cheryl, who is sixteen years old, was first taken to an ice-rink at the age of five. She found skating quite easy and quickly came to love it. She decided to make skating her career and went to a special sports school. She left at the age of fourteen and now studies two days a week with a private tutor. During the remaining five days, Cheryl travels to Aldershot Ice-Rink where she receives expert coaching. Cheryl has reached British Junior Standard and hopes to reach British Senior standard in the next two years. Her ambition is to represent Great Britain in the 1996 Winter Olympic Games.

I am an ice-skater. I arrive at the rink at about six o'clock in the morning, so I can have the ice to myself. I make sure my skating boots are laced very tightly.

Before I go onto the ice, I go through
a series of bending and stretching exercises.
A warm-up like this keeps me from straining
my muscles and joints as I skate.

After a few minutes, I remove the plastic guards from the blades of my skates. It is time to move onto the ice and continue my warm-up there.

In a competition, I have to perform a
series of compulsory figures and a
three minute program of free skating.
I start my practice by going through
my free skating routine.

I divide my program into short sections
which I practice one at a time.
I have to repeat difficult movements
many times before I can do them
well enough for competitions.

In a competition, equal marks are awarded for technical merit and artistic impression. During my practice I must work on both sides of my performance.

My coach watches each part of the routine.
She is always on the lookout for mistakes!

She gives me advice on how to improve
my technique.

My coach used to be an international skater so she can demonstrate exactly how every movement, such as this "inside spreadeagle," should be made.

She also helps me with my interpretation.
The way I hold my hands and head
can make all the difference between a
winning and a losing performance.

I perform several jumps during my program. I have to skate very fast to build up the speed I need to spin round in the air.

After practicing all the sections of my routine, the time has come for a complete performance. My coach puts on my music and I get ready to start.

My music is from a Broadway musical.
It is very catchy and so I try to match
the music with a lively performance.

I use graceful movements, such as this arabesque, when the music is slower.

I end my performance with a spin. I turn more slowly when my arms are outstretched.

As I draw my arms into my body, I spin much faster. Although I am used to spinning, I still feel slightly dizzy when I finish.

More about skating

Figure skating is divided into three kinds of competition — single skating, pair skating and ice dancing.

Single skaters give three types of performance:

Compulsory figures — Skaters have to trace accurate designs on the ice. These are based on figures of eight. Short program — Skaters perform a series of eight compulsory moves in whatever order they wish, to music. Long program — Skaters select and arrange a four minute program of their own movements, to music. The program is designed to show off their skating skills.

In pair skating, couples show how well they can skate together in a short program and a four minute free skating performance.

20

Lift

Waltz

Speedskater

Ice dancers combine some of the movements of ballroom dancing with skating. No high lifts are allowed and the couple must stay together as much as possible.

Speedskaters race over various distances on oval tracks. They reach speeds of 48 kph (30 mph).

Skates

Skating boots are made of stiff leather. They are laced tightly to support the ankles. The blades are screwed to the soles.

Blades are made of very high quality polished steel. The edges remain sharp even after skating for miles across hard ice.

Blades are ground to give them sharp edges which dig into the ice.

A jagged toe pick helps the skater jump, pivot and spin.

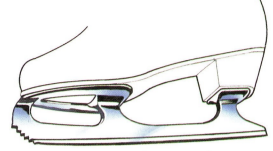

An ice dancing skate. It has a very short blade to allow close overlapping foot movements.

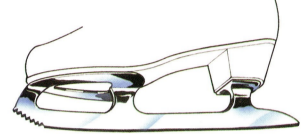

A figure skating blade. It has a shallow, hollow grind to allow smooth tracing. The toe pick is raised to allow the skater to cut cleaner figures.

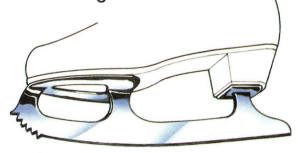

A free skating blade. The toe pick is placed up front, which is ideal for jumping. The long tail gives the skater better balance.

After lunch, I practice my figure skating.
My coach uses a scribe to
mark out some perfect circles on the
clean ice. These circles act as a
guide while I cut my own figures.

I have to cut smooth circles in the ice with the edges of my skates. The blades of my figure skates are much flatter than the blades of my free skates. These allow me to make flowing, clearly cut figures.

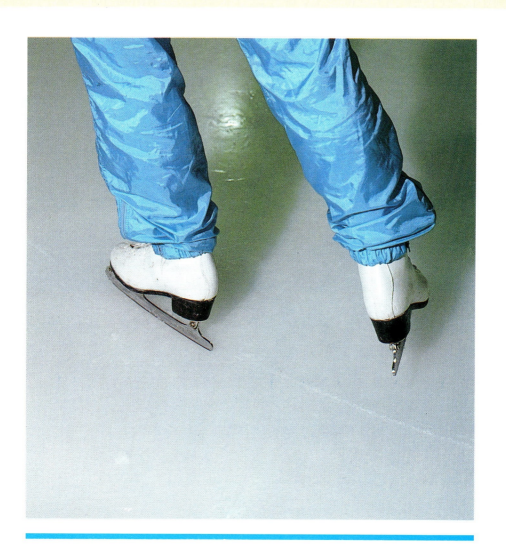

In a competition, each figure must be skated three times. I need total concentration and excellent control of my skates to re-trace a figure while still making the necessary turns 24 and changes of direction.

I need to be perfectly balanced to skate smoothly and to avoid cutting a wobbly line. My coach guides me to make sure my body is correctly positioned throughout the figure.

Here I am cutting the figure with my left skate. My coach makes a small change in the position of my free leg which should be carried with the heel over the tracing line.

I train for about forty hours each week. My coach checks my training schedule every day. I am about to take my National Skating Association silver medal test. This is the highest standard I can reach at junior level.

We're all nervous on the morning of the test.
My coach gives us a last minute briefing, and
then we go on to the ice one by one to take
the test in front of the official judges.

It's all over and I passed. Now I will have to work even harder to reach gold medal standard. Once I have done that, I can enter senior competitions and work towards the Olympic Games and the World Championships.

Facts about skating

The earliest known ice-skaters were the Romans. Excavations of Roman ruins in London have uncovered leather boots and ice-skates made of polished animal bones, which date from 50 BC.

The Vikings also used animal bones strapped to their shoes as skates. These early skates were used for transportation. During the 1300s, the Dutch used waxed wooden skates.

Steel blades on wooden soles appeared in about 1400.

The first all-steel skates were produced in The United States in 1850. They kept their sharp edges longer and helped to make skating a popular sport.

Figure skating was invented by an American ballet dancer, Jackson Haines, in about 1870.

Figure skating and speed skating became Olympic sports in 1924.

The greatest number of Olympic gold medals won by a figure skater is three by Gillis Grafström of Sweden and by Sonje Henie of Norway. The greatest number of world figure skating titles is ten by Ulrich Salchow, also of Sweden.

The highest points ever awarded to any skaters were given to Jayne Torvill and Christopher Dean at the World Ice Dance Championships in Ottawa, Canada in 1984. Their scores included twenty-nine perfect marks of 6.0. In their career, they were awarded a record total of 136 perfect marks.

GLOSSARY

Artistic impression
The way a skater expresses the mood of the music through his or her skating.

Compulsory figures
Designs which a skater must trace on the ice. They are designed to show that a skater has complete control over his or her movements. However, from 1990 onward they will be dropped from major competitions altogether.

Free skating
Skating where a skater selects his or her own sequence of movements, spins and jumps.

Ice dance
A type of pair skating which combines skating and ballroom dancing. During the dance the couple may separate only in order to change direction and position.

Program
The sequence of movements a skater will perform. Programs vary in length according to the competition and the level of the skater.

Scribe
A large metal arm, similar to a drawing compass, which marks perfect circles on the ice. Scribes are used to mark figures to guide skaters or to check how well a skater has traced a figure.

Technical merit
The accuracy with which a skater performs the moves.

Tracing
Cutting a mark in the ice with the skates. In compulsory figures skaters must trace clean figures on new ice, so the judges can see how accurately they have cut the figure.

INDEX